I0171519

Gyfted Ink LLC

Books may be purchased by contacting the publisher and author at:

gyftedink@gmail.com

Publisher: Gyfted Ink, a division of Gyfted Ink, LLC

Editor: Melissa Henry Stover

Creative Consultant: To God be the glory

Library of Congress Catalog Number: 2015907143

{Gyfted Ink LLC} {Lugoff, SC}

ISBN-13: 978-0692436332

ISBN-10: 0692436332

1. Spirituality 2. Self Help

First Edition   Printed In The US

The Thorn In My Flesh

BY STEPHANIE DYERS

4

Table of Contents

Parents

As I have journeyed through life, there is one thing that has always been constant, my family. You might say I am lucky. I just say I am well blessed. I have been placed in a family where love radiates and respect resides.

My mom is the picture of grace and elegance. Even though I was a tomboy, she still taught me how to be a lady. She did not allow her family to go out the house any kind of way. She knew you only had one chance to make a first impression. She also taught me life happens, go through your emotions but don't lay in them. You are the only one that can pick yourself up. Her favorite saying is "When life hands you lemons make lemonade".

Even though I look like my mom and have some of her ways, I am a daddy's girl. My Papa has always been my protector. He did not let anyone mess with his family. We were his most important and precious gems. Papa taught me all the things he thought I should know to take care of myself. You know the things like how to change a tire, check and change your oil, and to fix things around the house. It is great to have a man to depend on, but he knew I was going to leave his home one day, and

I had to be able to do some things for myself so I didn't get ripped off. My dad loved and still loves me with everything in him. Because we were so much alike we could talk for hours. Now we got into our fair share of disagreements but always found our way back pretty easy.

Even though, my parents were the best I could ask for. They could not shield me from the terrors of life. They could not watch me 24/7 and provide. Even though my Grandmother lived with us to help take care of my brother and myself, she could not shield us either. Children go through trials and tribulations just like everyone else. These same hardships and adventures shape us into who we are. It may not seem fair that God would allow such a thing, but it is all a part of His great plan. As we journey through this book together, you will understand more by and by. I give all honors to God. I also honor my parents because the things they taught me and enforcement of their rule of going to church has shaped me into the Woman of God I am today.

Introduction

In II Corinthians, Paul talks about the thorn in his flesh. He tells the church of Corinth how he asks for it to be removed. However, his request was denied. I can only imagine how Paul felt. We all have had some experience in our lives where we have asked for something only to be told no. As a child, I heard that word quite often. Not because my parents were mean; but because they knew what I was asking for didn't mean me any good. God's answer to Paul carries a purpose.

After reading and studying this subject, it became apparent to me that we all have

this thorn, but for the most part we choose not to discuss it. For years, scholars

have tried to figure out what this thorn was. Many have their suspicions, however,

no one but Paul and God truly knows. By Paul not revealing his thorn, it tells me that it does not matter what the thorn is. Paul was not a shy guy, so if it was

important, he would have revealed it. Maybe Paul didn't reveal it because he

knew

people and the consequences that could arise. I would have to believe it is a

combination of the two. I believe the thorn is not for publication but for

knowing

and understanding the purpose of it. Had Paul revealed his thorn, people who

read

his letters would have focused on the thorn and not the importance of the next

verse. God's reply which is …My grace is sufficient for you, for my power

works

best in weakness…(II Corinthians 12:9 NLT). I believe by the prompting of

the Holy Spirit, I have been given the task of showing my battle scars, but

most of

all revealing my thorn that others may better understand theirs and its

purposes.

MY TESTIMONY

I grew up in a family of much love. At the same time, I dealt with adult

issues early. From the age of five to eight, I was molested by two different

men, due to fear from those men, I never spoke about it. Then in my teen

years, I was raped and then rape a second time. Needless to say, I was not a

fan of men. My hatred for men just would not allow me to trust them. I tried

to date, but it seemed my attraction was stronger toward women. It was

probably stronger because just like a baby in a mother's womb has a placenta

for protection, women were mine. I have always been a tomboy, but it

seemed like I never grew out of that stage. I remember the first person who

asked me if I was gay. Of course I denied it. However, in my mind I was

pondering yes. Now I did not grow up with homosexuality freely displayed

around me. During the 80's and 90's, it was not common practice for gays

and lesbians to be out. So where did

this thought come from? I understand that doctors say there is a timeframe where all children question their sexuality. However, I was not questioning it. I was feeling it. With my family being such active members of the church, I was no stranger to the Word of God. I understood sinful acts but, I also understood God's compassion. What I did not understand was what to do. Like I said, I understood God's compassion, but people were a totally different thing. I was in all out warfare with myself, but who could I confess it to? The Bible states confess your faults one to another (James 5:16). But how do you confess your faults when you know you will be judged. With what I was feeling and with no one to talk to, I finally embraced the lifestyle. I was in it for about 10 years. However, I still felt torn in my spirit. People saw the outside person, the person that exuded confidence in what she did. I didn't care who liked it or not. But it was during the quiet times that I was torn; the times when I would fight within because even though I like the fleshly feelings, I did not like the spiritual feelings. Those are the real tests. Any person can put on the greatest show in public, but the times when it is just you and God, there is no smoke and mirrors, just mirrors.

By now, I didn't really go to church anymore. My thought was who want to feel judged in a place where love was supposed to radiate. Instead it became a place church folk would stare at you the entire service or point and whisper, because they did not agree with your attire or lifestyle. God forbid I try to hug and get close to any of the church folk. It was as if homosexuality was a disease that had no cure, or if I came in midst of any of these good old church folks whatever it was that possessed me was going to jump on them. I'm pretty sure a lot of people have felt this way. For some reason people want to rank sin. There is no sin hierarchy just sin. The sin is not the root of the issue but the symptoms of the issue. You know the demeanor attached to the sin. The pimp walks of a lesbian or flamboyance of homosexual, the shifty eyes of a liar, the visual arrogance of pride, or the sneakiness of a cheater. Since lesbianism had become my persona and could be seen from a mile away, that was all anyone saw. No one bothered to take the time to closely examine the root of my issue-brokenness. The bad part was, the ones that really cared about my soul were drowned out by the naysayers. The ones that told me God hated me, and I was an abomination to him and going to hell. Yes, the Bible does talk about abominations and the ultimate cost of sin is death. However, the important part left out was that God did not hate me, but He hated the sin.

By the time I was 20, I had lost my scholarship, dropped out of college, became a functioning alcoholic, indulging in drugs and living a homosexual life, but God has a way of reaching even those we think are unreachable. To this day, I still believe God sent a special friend into my life to help me. She always told me in our four years of living together that she was not gay. I never could understand until years later. Our meeting was inspired by God, due to circumstances and our flesh it went the wrong direction. However, only God can take a mess and still get

the glory out of it. Regardless, rather she knew it or not she was on a divine

mission for God.

The beginning of change

Finally, I hit an all time low. Having grown up in the church there was one

thing I always knew when you're in trouble, call on God. I dusted off my

bible and just began reading no

particular book, chapter, or verse. I just read. Then one morning it happened. As I was sitting in my bed watching T.V. with this lady, my arm was around her nothing unusual for me. I even remember the vase of roses on the window sill. Then it happened, it was as if a fist came down from heaven and hit me upside my head. It was intense; I could feel a big rattle inside my head if you have ever been hit before you know the feeling. Can you imagine the hand of God hitting you? I turned and looked at her and it was as if my eyes had been opened for the first time. I remember shockingly saying to myself, "I'm in bed with another woman." This unexplainable feeling came over me the next thing I knew I was taking my arm from around her and moving away. After that our relationship began to change. It was not an overnight thing, but it sure was the beginning. She was my last homosexual relationship. About a year or two later, we both reunited with Christ. Now after allowing God back into my life and through God's grace most all the thing I struggled with have been dismissed. I have overcome drugs, alcoholism, and promiscuity. However, homosexuality continued to be the thorn in my flesh. As an Evangelist, it is hard to admit this publicly because when ministers admit a weakness, we are ridiculed the more. People tend to forget those who minister the Word of God are still people of the flesh. We each work on putting our flesh under subjection through the Word of God just like every other person. Our lives are just looked at under the microscope closer. This is the reason why people should not place ANY individual on a pedestal. God forbid they are overtaken in sin. There is only one who walked this earth and did not sin. His name is Jesus. He is the ONLY one we should put on a pedestal because He will not fall or fail us. By now some of you may be ready to put this book down and say it is of demonic forces, but I encourage you to read on. This is truth. …They that worship must worship in spirit and in truth. (John 4:24 KJV) Let's face it; the truth is usually not gift wrapped in some pretty box with a nice bow on top of it. It actually is the ugliest present under the tree. For far too long, we have tried to make things sound good for the sake of others, but I believe God is ready for us to get real truthful. For years, I lived in denial. Telling myself that the urges were not there, and I tried my best to live as if it wasn't. The real truth is, I was not living. I lived my life in a bubble, keeping people at bay. Thinking, if I kept them far enough away there would be no chance of anything evolving. Then one day, I met one of the coolest people I could have ever met. The Christ in her began to love the walls I had built away. It was like sugar meeting water. The walls I had erected over time were melting quickly. However, in the mist of all this, my fear was becoming reality. I was again coming under attack. Those buried feelings began to arise. "How could this be?" I said, "No, this is not supposed to happen." The more I tried to hide it the worst it got. I began fight with and to doubt myself in God. How can I preach, teach, or witness to anyone when I have this issue? The enemy's tactic was working. He was making me feel ashamed of myself and I had done nothing wrong. Then I got

angry and had a conversation with God. I remember saying I thought I was

delivered from this. Doesn't deliverance mean no more it's gone? I have been

celibate for 10 years overcoming my addiction of sex. I have not done drugs

in almost the same amount of time. I can't stand the smell of cigarettes; they

make me sick to my stomach. Now God you have delivered me from all this

but, I'm not delivered from homosexuality?" Then God spoke to my spirit

and said something so profound to me. He said, deliverance does not always

mean full removal sometimes it is a choice. You are probably thinking…

What?! I did not

understand at the time either, but we will discuss that later.

As I stated earlier, I believe I have been prompted by the Holy Spirit to show

my battle scars in this book and reveal my thorn. By doing this, I pray with

God's

help people will get a broader understanding of deliverance, gain a little

more compassion, and realize each of us have a thorn in our flesh. I also pray

that people will recognize it, but most importantly understand the purpose of

the thorn because

in all our getting we must get understanding. (Prov. 4:7)

Thorn

Growing up, I loved roses. There was a little flower bed of roses along

the side of my parents' yard. I thought they were some of the most

beautiful flowers I had ever

seen. However, they were something I would learn to admire from a distance. When I was young, I decided I would try to pick one. I was naïve to fact something was sticking out of the stem, I just grabbed it. Now you know what happened. The pain I felt from the thorns was unforgettable. Even now, if I think of picking one, the memory comes back so vividly. Now, just as the thorns on roses serve a purpose, so does the thorn in our flesh. Whether we believe it or not, it has been put in place for our protection.

Our dear Brother Paul asked 3 times for his thorn to be removed. Each time he was denied and told, "My grace is all you need. My power works best in weakness... (II Corinthians 12:9) To some this may seem like a cruel act of God. If God loved us so much why would he allow something to torture us, but it is because he loves us so much. After all, this man served him dearly. He was always in somebody's jail cell, beaten many times, shipwrecked and stoned almost to death. He pretty much suffered the duration of his walk with God. (II Corinthians 11:23-28) God would not remove a simple thorn ? You may ask. No, He didn't! We know that God causes everything to work together for the good of those who love Him and are called according to His purpose. (Romans 8:28 NLT). If you look at the book of Job, he too had hardships, but he said though He slay me, yet will I trust Him… (Job 13:15)

In this chapter, I want us to take a closer look at the job of a thorn. After some research, I discovered that anything that has thorns or prickles are for protection. Animals are drawn to the sweet smell and taste of plants, so as a protection they have thorns. This is a real statement of God's love for all his creatures. He even gave the plants protection against those that desire to devour them. Matthew 6:25-30 talks about not worrying for tomorrow what we should eat, drink, or wear. He tells us to look at the birds they do not sow, reap, or gather, yet our heavenly Father feeds them. If God cares so much for the plants and animals to protect and feed them what wouldn't He do for us? These are real statements of God's love. So if He gave the plants protection against those that desires to devour them. Can you imagine what more he would do for us? If Jesus is our rock and shield and protector why would we need thorns? Who are we being protected from? Believe it or not we are being protected from ourselves. As Paul talks about this thorn in II Corinthians 12:7 he gives us the reason. Paul says it was given to him to keep him from becoming conceited or puffed up because of the surpassingly great revelations. As stated earlier, Paul went through some serious stuff. In today's society, we most likely would have a hard time handling these challenges. I believe some of us would have looked at our boss and said, "Naw man this right here is not going to work, I don't have to put up with this. I QUIT!!!" When I think of Paul, I consider him as a fool.

Yes, a fool for Christ. What else would you call a person who counted it joy to go through such endeavors? Think about it, if someone like Paul came up to you and told you some of the things he went through and then said count it all joy to endure suffering for the Name of Christ. You would hurry and commit him to the nearest mental institution.

After reading all the things Paul saw, I could see how he could become conceited. Some of us get puffed up because of the car we drive or the house we live in. What more revelations from God. It takes a lot of self control to have such great revelations and not become big headed. It would take everything we have or better yet, a simple thorn to keep us from walking around puffed up. That is the thing about pride, without something to keep us grounded it can destroy us. If you think because Paul was an apostle, was the reason he saw so many things and needed a thorn. You couldn't be farthest from the truth. We are all uniquely made. A title does not make one more special than another. We all have unique gifts and talents. The Bible tells us that gifts come without repentance (Roman 11:29) and God would withhold no good thing from us (Psalm 84:11) If we seek and ask Him. He will answer. God is no respecter of person and there is nothing so great about Brother Paul that only he received a thorn. He is just the only one who has confessed it.

It took a while for me to acknowledge my thorn, not because it was hidden but because I refused to acknowledge it. Who would have thought this dirty little secret, as some may put it, would be the very thing that keeps me grounded. The thing I prayed to be removed but God told me in his Word, my grace is sufficient for you; my strength is made perfect in weakness. This thorn causes me to rely on God because in my own strength, I would most likely still be with women. I was not strong enough to stop. The truth is as much as I wanted to stop; I could not do it alone. I needed someone more powerful than myself.

Here is an exercise for you. Look at yourself for one week. Don't focus on anyone but you. In fact, I give you permission to be selfish this week in order to find out your thorn. Some may not even need a week because you already know. It's the thing you may not want to acknowledge. The thing you sneak around and do in the dark or maybe something that no matter how many doctors you go the illness is not curable just livable. Maybe you are addicted to porn, desire the taste of alcohol or the feeling of getting high, never satisfied with what you have, or a compulsive liar. Maybe you're someone who is required to constantly intercede for the very one who desires your life or any number of things. There is no greater or lesser thorn. Just as every person is unique so will your own thorn be in your life. It has been customly made for you. I'm not asking you to share it but please remember it the next time you are ready to put someone on blast, be cruel, or exalt yourself higher, that it is God's grace and mercy that pulled you out. God knows each of us. His creations were made perfect. I pray you will remember your thorn and show compassion. As Jesus told the men ready to kill the woman caught in adultery. You that is without sin cast the first stone. (John 8:7)

My Grace Is Sufficient

In this chapter, I want to discuss God's answer to Paul about the removal of his thorn. As stated in the previous chapter, Paul asked three times for his thorn to be removed. However, God's answer was no. There are time when we will ask God a question and his answer is no. That can be very frustrating, but we must remember God knows what is best for us. He can see the future and He knows what we are able to handle (Corinthians 10; 13). One of the things I love about God is His answer of no because He gave a counter offer. No I will not remove that thorn but I will give you grace, that alone is sufficient. To the natural eye removal would be better, but to the spiritual eye grace is better. Grace is unmerited divine assistance given humans for their regeneration or sanctification (Merriam-Webster). God was telling Paul his grace or divine assistance was more than enough. God's power is perfect in our weakness. It is another example of how much we need God. We were never built to handle everything. Philippians 4:13 states I can do all things through Christ who strengthens me. The word all is so small yet so powerful. It is inclusive

to everything. We must put our strength in God and use His assistance

to make it. Peter was able to walk on water as long as his eyes stayed

focus on Jesus. It was when he lost focus he began to sink. I know for

myself that without God's assistance. I would not have been able to be

delivered out of homosexuality. Most of all I would not be able to stay

out. I do believe every person has encountered moments where they

become puffed up over something. It is a part of the human nature.

However, there is always something that can make every giant fall. For

Goliath it was one single stone slung by a little boy named David, but

guided by the hand of God. What humans call weak the Spirit call

strength. It takes more to admit weakness than strength, who wants to

be weak? I believe God gets excited when we admit our weakness to

Him. He now says rest in me and let me show what I can do for you. In

that very moment testimonies

are made. I have been blessed with a loving family. I am a daddy's girl, and I know I can lean on him in my weakest most venerable state. He is going to do all he is naturally able to do. Even when I say no I will figure it out. That is an example of a natural father's love. I can only imagine what more my Heavenly Father will do. Scriptures tell us human parents give good gifts to their children what more our Father in heaven. This is why Paul and everyone else can rest assured God's grace is sufficient. God's grace is revealed in our weakness. It is God's desire for us to depend on him. Our thorn serves as a constant reminder of this. God wants us to use his strength because it is perfect. Had it not been for Paul's thorn he may have never became the crusader he did. I'm not saying to be a weak person, but understand that in our weakness God gives us strength.

Deliverance

In this chapter, I want to discuss deliverance in more detail. Deliverance is

the key to understanding the thorn. As stated earlier, God let me know

deliverance is not just about removal but also a choice. For many years, we

have been told if the temptation of a thing has not been removed then you

have not been delivered, you need to pray harder. Throughout my Christian

walk, I have realized because of the feeling of guilt through condemnation,

people lived a double life. They really do love the Lord, but think if people in the church knew they were still battling the desires of sexual addiction, alcoholism or whatever else they wrestle with, they would be considered less holy. The worst part is that some don't even make it that far, they just go back into the world, because whatever they are struggling with is still there. They can't take the idea of feeling like they are not worthy of God's mercy. It is not God who feels this way but we, his representatives, who have given this false allusion. It is the label hypocrite that is used. As Christians, we sling this word around like fertilizer, growing hatred and misunderstanding. The true meaning of this word is often misused in the church. In classical Greek, it meant stage playing or acting. What is failed to be realized is when people are trying to do right by God and they are having issues; it does not make them hypocrites. The true hypocrites are those who show religion outwardly but inside are insincere and unrighteous. (Matthew 15:8) They are the ones pushing those God has drawn in through the front door out the back door. How dare we as Christians put someone in Hell? I have yet to know of anyone who has been given a copy of that key.

Revelations 1:18 states Jesus is the only one with keys to death and hell.

Matthew 16:19 Peter was given the keys to the kingdom of heaven and now

we too have those keys, but there is only one with the key to hell. It is in the

secure hands of Jesus only to be brought out at the Day of Judgment.

However, somehow we have been given a false key, made copies, and

distributed out to others. The dungeon that people have created and you have

been placed in is an allusion.I encourage you to just open the door and walk

out. There really is no lock on the door.

One day, I made a choice to open the door and walked out and live my life

for Christ. For years, I allowed what I wanted to be first, instead of what

God required of me based upon the biblical doctrine. Now, have I arrived?

Oh No! I strive everyday to do better than the day before. Sometimes I have

setbacks, but I repent from the heart and keep on moving forward.

Deliverance is not free it will cost you something. I think back to the story of Jacob's blessing in Genesis 32:22-32. He was in need of a blessing. He wrestled with a man. The bible says during this wrestling match he received a touch that dislocated his thigh socket. However, he continued to wrestle with a dislocated socket in his thigh until he received his blessing. The blessing Jacob received cost him. It cost him the ability to walk without a limp, but it was worth it to him. Just like that blessing cost Jacob it will also cost us, but the reward will be greater. Sometimes deliverance will cost you your so called friends, family, jobs, etc. It cost Jesus his natural life.

Many people believe deliverance came at the cross. However, I would like to be bold enough to say it began in Gethsemane. In Matthew 26:39, Mark 14:36, and Luke 22:42, all these scriptures say pretty much the same thing. Lord, if there is any other way for me to bring deliverance let me know, but Lord I love you more than me so your will be done. This was where deliverance began, with a choice made by Jesus to go through with the rest of the trial, death, and resurrection. He could have just walked away and said no this is too hard for me and you and I are not worth it. However, he chose to go on. This is why I have to believe everything is not dismissed or taken away. Jesus' pain was not taken away in fact the closer He got to bring full deliverance the pain became more intense. Take a moment to think over some things Jesus endured. Can you imagine being beaten with items that with every blow parts of your flesh is removed; having thorns embedded into your head until blood ran down or having nail, but not just any nails, spikes as used on a railroad driven into your feet and wrist, finally to be pierced in your side with a spear? Jesus was required to walk at least a half mile up the hill to Calvary carrying a huge cross. He was spit on and given sour vinegar instead of water; none of this was not done privately but publicly. This was a choice Jesus made to bring deliverance to the world. Just as the angels came and strengthened Jesus, they come and strengthen us when we too   are weak.

My battle with homosexuality may be something I fight with, but I know that in that time I must turn to the one who is able to strengthen me so I am able to overcome it. One key thing is everyone does not deal with their issues the same. For some of us who were once indulged in the gay life, they choose to live the rest of life in celibacy; some are blessed to have engaged in a healthy marriage. While some may still be in the life fighting to stop, that does not mean they don't love the Lord and are not trying to do His will. Like everything in life, people fall into temptations, but the key is to get up. Do not stay in it. If you are one of these that believe you cannot do it because the urges are to strong or that it is just how you are, I am sorry to burst the excuse bubble. When we were created we were created in perfect spirit. However, once we were clothed in flesh and blood, we were also clothed with the sins of the world. All have been born into sin and shaped in iniquity. Everyone born has a sinful nature just because of the skin we are in, literally.

However, our mind makes the final decisions not our limbs. They are

the accomplices. When a crime is committed the police may get the

accomplices, but they are after the mastermind. The person whose idea

it was. Just as the police go for the head, so must we. This is why it is

imperative to renew the mind everyday. Be careful of what enters the

ears and eyes. Those things shape the mind. If you want to stop

cussing, then stop listening to it. If you want to stop watching porn,

then stop allowing your eyes to see it. As I stated before there are

things God just took from me. Others I had to learn to make conscious

decisions not to engage in them. Even though it felt good to my flesh,

God showed me a way to escape it was up to me to choose to take it.

The temptation in your life is no different from what other experience.

And God is faithful. He will not allow the temptation to be more than

you can stand. When you are

tempted, he will show you a way out (1 Corinthians 10:13 NLT). I believe everything we do wrong there is a pull or hesitation within us. If you take a moment and just think back to the first time you committed any wrong act, you will remember the hesitation. That hesitation is the spirit within us telling us" no don't do it". But we override it with our own reasoning. Have you ever watched a small child that has never been told something is wrong, the first time they do that act they will look around to see if anyone is looking? Even though they are unable to understand the spirit within, they know something. It starts just that early. I have spoken a lot about the mind because that is where the choice is made. God never holds us hostage to His will. He just offers rewards and punishment. The same thing parents, judges, or people with authority do. Choosing to do right by God's standards, that is a true test of your love for Him. It is easy to stop doing things we no longer like or have the urge to do, but it is true love for God to deny ourselves things we love to do that is not pleasing to God. The reward of such great sacrifice will be overflowing and unable to be contained. I pray today you make a choice to be delivered.

Church Folks

Earlier in the book, I stated how there were people who were truly out to encourage my soul, but I could not receive their help due to all the naysayers. I believe everyone who calls themselves Christians are not, but are really church folk. What's the difference? Christians and church folks both believe in

God. However, one has a relationship with God and the other has more religion than relationship. Old Testament calls these people Pharisees.

The bible states in Matthew 7:21-23 everyone who says Lord Lord will not enter the kingdom of heaven. There are people who can heal, preach, prophesy, and many other things through God's gift. However, just because they can do them, does not mean they will enter into heaven. They will find themselves in the Lake of Fire. We must learn to have a love and compassion to others. Tell people the Word of God, but then allow His Word to do the work. The bible states that we should be careful least we fall. There was a time in my life in which I was at that point. I had become so heavenly minded I was of no earthly good. My bile of compassion was shut up. I began to do to others what people had done to me. I was one good step from a major fall.

Sins are committed all day long everyday, from the front door of the church to the pulpit. I concluded that I would rather be a sinner in church and know it,

working to get right than to be in the church acting like what someone

else did was worse or yet like I did nothing at all. There is no hierarchy

in sin. All sin is created equal, and receives the same wages, death.

After I got saved, I began to really condemn people from a harsh point.

Not because I was mean but because my passion over ruled my

compassion. I just wanted people to see God like I did. But in my

efforts I came off condescending and alienating rather that drawing. I

was really on fire for God. Every Saturday night, I was at Bible Study

and every Sunday in church. If you came in my pathway you heard

about God. You would think it was great, and it was, until I went into

religious mode. There is a thin line between telling the goodness of

God verses religion. I no longer focused on telling people how good

God was and what He did for me. Instead I began telling them

everything they were doing

contrary to the Word, and it wasn't even in a loving way. I was acting as if I had become the picture perfect Christian. Unbeknownst to myself I had fallen to scripture. I was trying to pull the splinter out of someone else eye and yet having the beam in my own eye.(Matthew 7:3) At the time it was my belief that females should not wear pants, had to wear head coverings, could not wear gold jewelry nor celebrate any holidays or birthdays. It was two year later before God opened my eyes and revealed his grace through His Word. I could remember being at work telling ladies what they should and should not do. Needless to say I lost ground with these people. Then, I told my mom it was not right to go to family reunions. She was already dealing with a lot from me with my new found religion, but when I told her that, her words to me were " wait just a minute you have just gone to far now." My mom is a quiet lady so it takes a lot to rile her up, but if you do, watch out! I did not realize had offended her. All because of my interpretations of the scriptures were skewed.

She often takes things to God in her secret place. I can only imagine

what she prayed for me that day. I do know whatever it was God heard

and honored.

My dad, who is a pastor, and I were constantly disagreeing. We would

be disagreeing about how to baptize, celebrate holidays, birthdays, and

other religious stuff nothing that really needed to save souls. But these

were things my family had been doing for years. Now all of a

suddenly, I gained a little knowledge, or so I thought, like I had

become the Guru on God. However through all this chaos, it was my

dad who actually showed me the way. Not by words but actions. It was

Christmas time and even though I was not celebrating at the time, my

brother and his family were coming home. By the request of my

Grandmother, I went home. I was home for about two or three days. I

probably had a debate with

everyone in the house except the babies. The day before Christmas, the family went out to do their last minute shopping. I went with them. My dad and I were in this Christian bookstore and he looks over at me and says, "I see something I think you need." It is not a Christmas present just something I see you need. Then he asked me if he could get it. I really did not know what to say but eventually muddled out a yes. He then handed me a bible cover. This had nothing to do with the bible cover. It was his actions toward me. Here I was debating like a mad woman and he still found it in his heart to do something for me and still respect what I was doing. Christmas morning was the clincher. I sat in the kitchen while everyone opened their gifts. Even though I didn't participate I still enjoyed watching the expressions on everyone's face when they opened their gifts, especially the kids. After all the opening was over, I sat in my parents' office. My dad came in and sat next to me. He said, "God has given me an understanding for what you are doing and I respect that." I remember hugging him as if I had seen him for the first time in years. What my dad showed me more than anything was his Christ-like nature. Where I was trying to give religious laws; he was showing Godly love. Love trumps law every time. I thank God for showing me the way, but it was a process. I believe that was when I really began to understand loving was better than pointing as I went through my next life lesson.

When I moved to the valley of the sun, Arizona, I was in a backslidden state. I'd stop going to church because I didn't want to feel like I was mocking God by coming to church on Sunday after rolling out of bed with someone who was not my spouse or just coming in from the club. Isn't it funny how the enemy tricks us with this excuse? How could I mock God by going to church, that is a tactic of the enemy to get us away from the very thing we need at that time. But God has a way of drawing you to Himself as only he could do. I started attending this church and one day, I was inspired to give my testimony. Actually, I never knew I was giving it until it was said. Out of my mouth like a rocket comes the confession. I use to live a homosexual lifestyle. Boy, you could have heard a pin drop in that place. I felt a need to repeat it. By this time, I'm thinking in my head what just happened and did I really just say what I thought I said. By then it was too late to back pedal. So I continued on. After giving this testimony, people changed toward me, not every one but some. In fact, that was the day I really accepted my call into the ministry. I needed to talk to someone so I went to my Pastor the same day to inform them I needed to discuss something. I was given a meeting time. Well the Pastor did not show for the meeting. I didn't sweat it, but I wanted to do a praise dance that following Sunday. I informed the correct people and they were onboard but had to run it past Pastor. When the gentleman discussed it, the Lord opened my ears to hear the conversation five rows away. The Pastor said no. Now the pastor was willing for me to do one before the testimony so what could have changed? I was considered unfit to do it and put someone else in my place. Needless to say I was hurt, but still pushed forward. I went over after service to greet as I usually did. I reached out to give a hug as we always did. The hug I received was cold and void of feelings. It took me for a loop. In my mind I was thinking is this the same person who was ranting and raving about me just a couple of weeks earlier? The same person who showed me such love before? I could not believe it. I tried to give the benefit of the doubt that it was an off night, but as I watched the interaction with others I knew I was not wrong. The only thing that could have changed was they knew my past. The cycle started all over again and I did not go to that church for a while. I was having hurt feelings from someone I adored because they knew my past. I was not as strong in my Christian walk as I am now. I did face this again years later, but held the faith and refused to allow others to make me walk away from God. When I did return to that church, the topic was generational curses. The subtopic of sexual deviants came up. The guest Preacher asked for those who wanted prayer, suffered or knew someone who suffered from this issue to come up prayer. I go up knowing prayer would help strengthen me and for others I knew. Suddenly, the Pastor took the microphone and began saying things in reference to my past and then asked me to repeat some words. I can't remember to this day what they were, but I do know I repeated in obedience. Now there was about seven or eight of us standing there, but I was the only one pointed out and not in a good way. Of course I was very embarrassed. How I wish it would have stopped there. At the end of the service, I was confronted again in front

of the congregation. Everything in me wanted to run, but God would

not let me. It was as if my feet were glued to the floor. All I could do

was smile and hold back the tears. As I was trying to leave, two more

women approached me and said, "I am woman hear me roar." Now

what did that have to do with anything? I don't know. This is a prime

example of God's drawing in the front door and people pushing you

out the back door. I hold no ill feelings now, but see it as God's way

of moving me to my next level. I must admit before things started

falling apart, I did receive some great healing of other deep wounds.

Romans 14:3 say so let's stop condemning each other. Decide instead

to live in such a way that you will not cause another believer to

stumble and fall.(NLT) When hurting people come in the church they

don't need us to hurt them more. Yes, there will be times when each of

us will hurt another, but if we

cannot admonish in love then let us just keep our mouths closed. None of us have the keys to hell and death, so what right do we have to try and place people there or keep them locked in their past. When I was living a homosexual lifestyle, I don't believe many people would have believed I would be an Evangelist today. They only saw the broken me at that time, but God know the plans he has for me (Jeremiah 29:11). The good part is had I not gone through what I did, I could not testify of it or how God brought me out. I know all thing work to my good. (Romans 8:28) I encourage everyone take a long look at yourself check and see if you are a Christian or a church folk. Don't know how to check? Here may be some indications for you. Are you jumping up and down, running around the church shouting hallelujah and falling out gracefully during church and then turning around after the benediction to say to someone I can't believe sister or brother so and so came in here wearing that. The must have come straight from the club. Look a there, you know she is sleeping with thus and thus and don't even know who none of those baby's daddies are. Woo Wee, I saw deacon at the liquor store Friday afternoon. I wonder if he was drunk in here today. I can't believe that man is singing in the choir. Everybody knows he goes that way. If these are some statements you may be making you may just be church folk. . Church folks are people who have a tendency to be judgmental and making statement like these. If you realize this maybe you go to God, and He will guide you on how and what to say to encourage. Now, if you are thankful just to see them in church, go over and embrace them and let them know God loves them and have a purpose for their life. You are a Christian. Jesus died on the cross for our sins, but before he did he showed us how to love, show compassion and forgive. He is the ultimate example of love, compassion and kindness.

To my sisters and brothers struggling with issues and choosing not to

go to church because you feel that you are mocking God. You are not.

That is not the definition of mocking God. As I have heard pastors say

before just keep coming God is shaping you each time. I do encourage

you to pray and ask God to lead you to a place where His true Word is

taught. Yes, if you're in the right place, The Word will cut, but it will

also heal you because that is what it is designed to do, and the people

of God will love you as your wounds heal.

CONCLUSION

As we have journeyed through my life, I pray you have received some

enlightenment on compassion but most of all the thorn in your flesh. My

thorn seemed to overshadow my life and if I do not stay focus in God's Word

it still will. I know I will not be able

to please all people. Certain ones will always condemn me. They will never see me as delivered. To them, I will always be" the dyke" in the pulpit as it has been put it. However, it is not any person's approval I am looking for any more only God's. Only things that are done for God will last. Everything else will eventually fade away. Even though, I have been given this thorn, I understand now, it is to keep me close to God for without Him I would be lost in my sinful life. The best choice I have ever made in this life was to give control of my life over to God. I may not understand everything He does but I am sure better off now than I was.

I want to extend to you the invitation given to me to accept the Lord Jesus as your personal Savior. Open your heart and say I admit I am a sinner. I believe Jesus Christ is Lord. He died for my sins and rose again with all power in His hand. Now because of your confession, faith, and belief in God your slate has been wiped clean. You are now a new creature in Christ Jesus. Your next important step is to find a bible base church where you are able to be baptized and learn of Jesus. You are now on a new journey. Let's walk it together.

GOD BLESS YOU AND MAY HEAVEN SMILE UPON YOU!